When Mama Ain't Happy, Ain't Nobody Happy

52 SECRETS UNCOVERED!
RULES THAT WOMEN
WANT MEN TO KNOW

Kris & Brian Gillespie

When Mama Ain't Happy, Ain't Nobody Happy
by Kris & Brian Gillespie

Published by
Insight Publishing Group
8801 S. Yale Ave. Suite 410
Tulsa, OK 74137

International Standard Book Number: 1-890900-33-8
Library of Congress Catalog Number:99-76083

This book is dedicated to . . .

my lovely wife, Kris, without whom I would never be where I am today.

and to our children, Michael, Jackson, and Catherine. A father could never have received better children than you.

I love you all very much.

ACKNOWLEDGEMENTS

First, I would like to thank my wife, Kris, for all the support she has given me in the development and writing of this book. In addition to giving me tremendous insight and feedback, she has maintained a great sense of humor through it all. Kris, I love you more than anyone I have ever known on this earth, and I cherish my time with you. After fourteen years of wonderful marriage, I can only look forward to what we have together.

I would also like to thank my parents, Pat and Bud Gillespie, and my in-laws, Lillian and Jack Jackson. Other than the obvious fact that neither Kris nor I would be here without them, their support for us has been tremendous through the years. Your input on the book was inspirational. I thank God for having such wonderful parents, and equally thankful that my wife came from such wonderful parents as well.

Thank you to the many friends and family that also provided great input on the book. Thanks go to Star and Dipo Aluko, Flo and David Caramela, Maureen Gillespie, Sid and Tracy Katchum, Roma and Brian Klemmer, Cheryl and Kevin Leslie, Cynthia and Kenny McGee, and Linda and Ray Ramon.

Thanks to Jim Shahin for providing excellent input and editing on this book.

Special thanks to Joseph V. Fiacco for the illustrations in this book.

Thanks to John Mason for his support of publishing this project.

No man is an island. I thank each one of you for your support in making this book a reality.

INTRODUCTION

When I married my wonderful wife in 1985, I had the sense that she knew something I didn't (in fact my wife still knows many things I don't yet have a clue about). Over time, I discovered that there were a set of unspoken "rules" in our household. Being a quick study, I learned the rules and adhered to them as much as I could, because the number one rule I discovered was, "when mama ain't happy, ain't nobody happy."

When our beautiful children began arriving in 1988, I was determined to be a good father, as I had been a good husband. I knew that my role was to teach my children the rules of a happy household. Each of these rules come from the number one rule, and must be adhered to for that harmonious home we all seek.

I limited my rule teaching activities to my children for two reasons. First of all, my primary concern is my wife and my children. But secondly, I assumed that everyone else knew the rules and that I was the only clueless one around. Not wishing to embarrass myself, I kept my mouth shut.

Then one day, I was speaking to a newlywed who described some situations she was facing with her new spouse. They certainly weren't serious in any regard, but it became clear that this gentleman didn't understand the rules. When I asked her if she had explained the rules to him, she asked me, "What rules?" All of a sudden, I didn't feel so clueless.

After explaining several of the rules, she gave me a

positive response. Confirmation, in my mind, that she recognized the rules, but had never had them articulated. Later, at dinner, with some other colleagues, I expounded on the rules some more. Out of that dinner came the suggestion for this book.

Of course, you can't just write a book like this without some input (better put, approval) from the woman of the house. In my case, this is my lovely wife, Kris, the adored "Mama" of our household. After receiving approval (I mean input), I embarked to detail the rules, as I know them. Each rule and explanation has received the stamp of authenticity of Kris. In other words, these are the official rules of our household.

My hope in writing this book is that I can save many men the confusion and disorientation that I went through in the first few years of marriage not knowing that there were rules. I hope that they will find, as I have, that the recognition of the rules and strict adherence to them, can significantly improve the quality of life at home. In other words, we get in trouble less, and our wives are happier.

Before you begin to take this book too seriously and begin to write letters to the publisher, or worse yet, me, let me give you our standard disclaimers.

This book is meant to be humorous. The best humor contains some truth and some fiction. As an intelligent human being, it is up to you to decide which is which. If you can't take a joke, stop reading this now. (In fact, you have probably already read too much for your own good.)

If you try this and it doesn't work in your house, don't blame me! These rules have been thoroughly tested and approved for my home only. While others have attested to these rules in their homes, I do not provide any guarantees, warranties or money back returns. In other words, there is a risk to everything, even drinking water.

If you try this and it doesn't work for you, ask your

wife to explain the rules to you. Just as every state has the same laws, but different applications of those laws, your home may use these laws different than mine. I know as men, we don't like to ask for directions or read instructions, but doing so in this case will produce great benefits for you. (Your wife will tell you the same thing about asking for directions or reading instructions.)

If you find these rules work in your home, teach them to your children by example. The truly happy home is happiest when everyone abides by the rules.

Be on the lookout for rule changes. Just like alternate side of the street parking regulations in New York City, rules can change depending on criteria that we don't fully understand. You must learn to read those confusing signs in order to avoid getting ticketed or towed (to the doghouse).

ABOUT MAMA

If you were to speak to Kris, the "Mama" of our home, she would likely tell you that these rules don't apply in our house. However, after further questioning, you could probably get her to admit that these rules do apply. She will offer you the caveat that, while the rules do apply, I don't adhere to them all of the time. To this statement, I would plead guilty.

In reading this book, you will get the impression that Kris has a tremendous sense of humor. My friends tell me they knew that when they found out that she was going to marry me. It is because Kris has this sense of humor that I am able to write this book.

Kris is the most wonderful, supportive, and inspirational woman I know. Throughout the writing of this book, she has worked with me closely to clarify the rules, distinguish what are real rules (versus what I hoped would be rules), and generally put up with my behavior while I worked on this book. To her, I am forever grateful.

One of my objectives in life is to be a great husband. It is in this pursuit that I have endeavored to discover and understand the rules written in this book. I fully expect that now that this is completed, with Kris as my teacher I will embark on developing the other rules I have missed. After all, my life's ambition is to Make Mama Happy (see Rule #28).

Rule #1

WHEN MAMA AIN'T HAPPY, AIN'T NOBODY HAPPY.

When Mama Ain't Happy . . .

Rule Application

Not only is this the title to the book, this is the number one, numero uno, primo, foundational rule. This rule stems from the influence that a wife and/or mother has on setting the atmosphere in the house.

How many men have walked into their home to find the atmosphere tense, without a clue about why it's tense. Men, I will give you the answer, *Mama ain't happy.* I know this is a revelation for some men, because it was for me one day. But I figured it out, and so can you. For whatever reason, when your wife is tense, you can feel it throughout the home.

The only answer to this is to make Mama happy. To make Mama happy, you need to find out what made her unhappy. I will give you another valuable answer as you ponder this. *Mama ain't happy because someone broke a rule.* Recognizing this, you have to make it right quickly. The faster you fix the situation, the faster you, too, can be happy again.

The rules listed in this book will help you regain that happy household. Now don't ask me how to apply these rules and fixes in your household; you have to figure that out. For the price you paid for this book, you can't expect everything.

WHAT TO DO WHEN THE RULE HAS BEEN BROKEN: DON'T BREAK THE MOST SACRED OF RULES. IF YOU DO, FIX IT FAST.

. . . Ain't Nobody Happy

Rule #2

THE RULE OF TWO: WHENEVER YOU DO SOMETHING WRONG, YOU MUST DO THE RIGHT THING TWICE FOR EVERY TIME YOU DID IT WRONG TO BREAK EVEN.

Rule Application

Whenever you break a rule, you must create situations where you adhere to the rule. When you do this twice, it takes away any penalty for breaking the rule the first time.

Example: You have just forgotten to buy your wife a gift for your anniversary. You worked late, and the stores were closed (sure you know you shouldn't have waited until the last minute, but it's too late for that now). The rest is history. The best way out is to buy a gift for your wife the next day—make it a very nice gift, preferably with flowers. As a surprise, buy her another (very nice) gift the day after or that weekend. This will get you out of the doghouse and forgiven.

WHAT TO DO WHEN THE RULE IS BROKEN: LIKE GRAVITY, THIS IS A RULE YOU CAN TRY TO RESIST, BUT THE FORCE OF NATURE IS TOO STRONG. LEARN TO WORK WITH IT. NATURAL LAWS WORK BEST WHEN YOU UNDERSTAND THEM, AND LEARN HOW TO USE THEM TO YOUR ADVANTAGE.

Rule #3

"WINNING" IS NOT A CONCEPT THAT WORKS IN MARRIAGE.

Rule Application

Someone once asked me, "How do I win in a discussion with my wife?" First the premise is wrong. There is no "winning." Winning is male thinking that will eventually get you into trouble. The more you try to win, the more your wife will make sure you lose. You may win the battle (argument), but lose the war (boy, it sure is cold in here).

Your wife is not thinking about winning. She is thinking about how to get to a place where you both feel good. If you must think about winning, define it as this place—where you both win.

WHAT TO DO WHEN THE RULE IS BROKEN: ABDICATE VIC-TORY. IT IS THE BEST WAY TO SHOW YOUR WIFE THAT SHE IS MORE IMPORTANT THAN WINNING.

Rule #4

WHATEVER CHORES YOU DO AT THE BEGINNING OF YOUR MARRIAGE, PLAN ON DOING THEM FOR LIFE.

Rule Application

(Warning: This rule may change during pregnancy.) Have you ever wondered how come you are stuck with the chores you have? The answer is simple. It all started the first day of your marriage. When you decided to do the dishes, you decided to do them for life. You may get your children to do them for the short period of time they are at home, but when they leave, it's your chore again.

This is not meant to be negative. You have to do chores. I am just warning you to chose carefully at the beginning.

WHAT TO DO WHEN THE RULE IS BROKEN: THE ONLY WAY TO GET OUT OF A CHORE IS TO NEGOTIATE A SWAP.

Rule #5

A HUSBAND'S ROLE IN THE DELIVERY ROOM IS TO UNDERSTAND HIS ROLE IN THE BIRTHING PROCESS IS NOT IMPORTANT RELATIVE TO HIS WIFE'S, AND THAT HE NEEDS TO SPEND THE REST OF HIS LIFE MAKING RESTITUTION FOR THAT FACT.

Personal Story: When our first child was born, I noticed something happening in the birthing room. The nurses, doctor, and my wife (all women), had very important jobs essential to the safe delivery of our beloved baby. About half way through, I noticed that my job was to tell my wife how to do something she already knew how to do, breathe.

At that time, I fully understood why men were expected to be in the delivery room. It is to bring into focus how limited our role is in the process, and how much our wives go through to bring our children into the world.

Rule Application

A husband has one important function in the nine-month childbearing process—he is expected to be there.

WHAT TO DO WHEN THE RULE HAS BEEN BROKEN: ONE OF THE WORST THINGS THAT YOU CAN DO AS A MAN, IS TO MISS BEING THERE FOR THE BIRTH OF YOUR CHILD. ALTHOUGH, IT IS A WONDERFUL AND MIRACULOUS EXPERIENCE, MEN CAN LIVE WITHOUT IT. WHAT YOU WILL FIND HARDER TO LIVE WITH IS YOUR WIFE'S CONSTANT REMINDER——FOR THE REST OF YOUR LIFE——THAT YOU MISSED THE BLESSED EVENT.

You see, when you aren't in the birthing room, you give your wife permission to hold this over your head for the rest of your natural (or that may be unnatural) life. The only thing that you can do at this point is to agree with her when she brings it up and say something like, "Honey, if it were up to me, I would have given birth to our children myself just to save you the pain and suffering." As insincere as everyone knows this is, it can't be refuted—because it will never happen.

. . . Ain't Nobody Happy

Rule #6

GOING SHOPPING WITH YOUR WIFE IS LIKE BEING SEVENTEEN DURING ELECTION YEAR. YOU CAN HAVE ALL THE OPINIONS YOU WANT, BUT YOU CAN'T VOTE.

Rule Application

Every man has been through it. You are shopping for furniture, carpets, or some household items. Your wife asks you what you think. Immediately, you think your opinion will impact the final outcome. WRONG!

You see, your wife is asking you to get another perspective, as limited as yours is. She already knows that you will learn to adapt to whatever she picks out, and will come to the understanding that she has much better taste than you.

Just think—how many times has someone complimented your wife on something in your house where the reply was, "My husband picked that out."

WHAT TO DO WHEN THE RULE IS BROKEN: EVERY MAN I KNOW HAS BROKEN THIS RULE AT LEAST ONCE. WE BEGIN TO HAVE A DISCUSSION (USUALLY IN THE STORE—OH BOY!) ABOUT WHAT WE THINK. IF YOU CATCH YOURSELF QUICKLY, TELL YOUR WIFE SOMETHING LIKE, "I'M SORRY. YOU'RE RIGHT, YOU HAVE A BETTER EYE THAN I DO FOR THIS TYPE OF THING."

If you don't catch yourself, and somehow that piece of furniture makes it into your home—get rid of it quickly! It will serve as a constant reminder to your wife that you broke the rule! The only way to get out of this is to give it away. Take your lumps early. Payback has interest!

. . . Ain't Nobody Happy

Rule #7

THERE IS NO SUCH THING AS WOMEN'S WORK. THERE IS WORK THAT IS SHARED, AND THEN THERE IS MEN'S WORK.

Rule Application

Cooking, washing dishes, vacuuming, laundry, cleaning toilets, and such are unisex chores. Everyone shares in the dirty work. (Remember to teach this to your children, especially your sons.)

On the other hand, taking out the garbage, lawn work, fixing the car, home repairs are chores for men. Sure, you didn't ask for it, but that's the way it works. Equality only goes so far.

WHAT TO DO WHEN THE RULE IS BROKEN: THE WORST THING YOU CAN DO IS TO IMPLICITLY EXPECT YOUR WIFE TO DO CERTAIN CHORES. THIS REEKS OF CHAUVINISM, WHICH COMES WITH MANDATORY SENTENCING. (IN OTHER WORDS, YOU AUTOMATICALLY HAVE TO DO THAT CHORE UNTIL YOU GET IT INTO YOUR THICK SKULL THAT THERE IS NOT SUCH THING AS WOMEN'S WORK.) IF YOU CATCH YOURSELF, PRONOUNCE SENTENCE ON YOURSELF. THIS WILL GO A LONG WAY IN REDUCING YOUR TIME.

A much less heinous crime is expecting your wife to help you with the men's work. Here, you just have to put up with a smirk or a disgusted look. This should be enough for you to get the hint.

A solution that works for everyone is to hire out chores that neither one of you likes to do. Having someone come in once a week to clean the house can keep both of you away from the dreaded bathroom chores.

Rule #8

WHEN LOOKING AT OTHER WOMEN, THE THREE-SECOND RULE APPLIES.

Rule Application

In basketball, there is the three-second rule. You can't be in the paint for more that three consecutive seconds. If you are, and you are caught, you will get called for a violation.

Most men are people watchers. However, there is a limit to how long you can watch. This rule applies mainly, if not strictly, to other women. Looking is OK. But looking that goes beyond three seconds is considered staring. Staring is a serious violation. If you get caught, you will be called for the violation.

WHAT TO DO WHEN THE RULE IS BROKEN: YOU WILL KNOW IF YOU HAVE VIOLATED THIS RULE BY THE LOOK ON YOUR WIFE'S FACE. THE BEST THING TO DO IS TO SPEAK QUICKLY. "YOU KNOW, I THINK THAT YOU WOULD LOOK MUCH BETTER IN THAT DRESS THAT SHE DOES." "DO YOU THINK THOSE SHOES GO WITH THAT DRESS?" "DON'T YOU THINK SHE SHOULD ACCESSORIZE BETTER?" THESE WON'T NECESSARILY GET YOU OUT OF TROUBLE, BUT IT WILL SURELY SOFTEN THE BLOW.

Rule #9

NEVER WHISTLE WHILE YOU PACK.

Rule Application

Business is not supposed to be fun. Leaving home on business is not supposed to bring you joy. Now we all know that some trips can be fun, and we actually look forward to that. You just can't let it show.

This is some sage advice I received from a friend of mine some time ago. He received it from a friend of his, and now I am offering it to you. It rang true then, and is still true today.

WHAT TO DO WHEN THE RULE IS BROKEN: MISERY. REMEMBER THAT WORD. MISERY IS THE ONLY THING THAT CAN GET YOU OUT OF THIS. WHEN YOU SPEAK TO YOUR WIFE ON THE PHONE TELL HER, "I THOUGHT THIS WOULD BE FUN, BUT WITHOUT YOU I AM MISERABLE." HOW'S THE WEATHER? "MISERABLE." HOW'S THE FOOD? "MISERABLE." ANYWAY, YOU GET THE IDEA.

. . . Ain't Nobody Happy

Rule #10

PUT THE TOILET SEAT DOWN, BUT NOT THE LID.

When Mama Ain't Happy . . .

Rule Application

A common complaint in many a household is that the males of the house don't put the toilet seat down. In the dark of the night, when a woman goes to answer the call of nature, the last thing she wants is a little extra water on her backside. And if she gets it, you will know.

What I never realized was that there was a rule for the lid as well. I figured, if you are going to put the seat down, put the lid down. That way, you don't have the unsightly view of the inside of the toilet. I was wrong. The rule is, toilet seat down, lid up. Don't ask me why, that is just the way it is.

Many women think that men should learn to pee sitting down. I know it sounds silly, even unmasculine. I don't support this, but in the interest of honesty, I thought I would let you know.

WHAT TO DO WHEN THE RULE IS BROKEN: FIRST, DON'T LAUGH. SECOND, APOLOGIZE PROFUSELY. THIRD, DON'T MAKE THE MISTAKE AGAIN. YOU MAY HAVE TO WONDER WHERE YOUR BATHROOM GLASS HAS BEEN.

Rule #11

THE TOTAL PURCHASE COST FOR
YOUR WIFE'S NEW CLOTHES MUST
INCLUDE THE MONEY TO TAKE
YOUR WIFE OUT TO SHOW THEM
OFF.

Rule Application

Your wife buys clothes to look nice. What is the sense of buying clothes if you can't show them off? Besides, it makes you look good, too.

When you buy a "guy" thing: stereo, TV, car, you like to show these off to your friends. The same holds true for your wife. She likes to show her stuff off as well.

So when your wife buys something for herself, look at the price tag and add a dinner to it. Call it the hidden tax you weren't told about (until now).

WHAT TO DO WHEN THE RULE IS BROKEN: DON'T FIGHT IT. TAKE YOUR WIFE OUT AND HAVE FUN. DON'T FORGET TO COMPLIMENT HER ON HOW GOOD SHE LOOKS. AFTER ALL, SHE IS DOING IT FOR YOU.

Rule #12

IF YOU BUY A GIFT FOR YOUR WIFE THAT YOU CAN USE, IT DOESN'T COUNT.

Rule Application

Everyone hears about the man who gets his wife a toaster, or something like that, for her birthday. That man is breaking this rule.

Women expect a gift to be something for them, which means you can't use it. You can't wear her clothes, jewelry, shoes, perfume or many other things. These are gifts. Stereos, TVs, pool tables, kitchen appliances are not. A gift is something she doesn't have to share. Period.

WHAT TO DO WHEN THE RULE IS BROKEN: YOU HAVE ONLY ONE OPTION. GO GET ANOTHER GIFT. (A REAL GIFT, THIS TIME.)

Rule #13

IF YOU BUY YOUR WIFE A GIFT
AND GIVE IT TO HER ONE WEEK
OR MORE AHEAD OF THE OCCA-
SION, IT DOESN'T COUNT.

Personal Story: For our thirteenth anniversary, I decided to buy my wife two diamond ring guards to complement her engagement ring, (which had seven diamonds from our seventh wedding anniversary). Because we had discussed ring style, patterns and such, we knew what we were going to get.

A month before our anniversary, my wife found ring guards that were on sale. She asked if we could get them early to take advantage of the sale. Always interested in saving money, I agreed and we bought the rings. I remember clearly stating that this was her anniversary gift. Equally clearly, I remember her saying yes.

Needless to say, a week before our anniversary, Kris began to drop hints about what she wanted for our anniversary. When reminded that she was wearing a very expensive gift, she gave me that puppy dog look (that we are all familiar with). I should have known better. I went out and bought her another gift.

Rule Application

We have all been in a situation where our wives find something that they really want, but that special day isn't for another few weeks. Her suggestion is, "Buy it for me now, and it will count as a gift." It's a trap!

When it comes time to celebrate that occasion and you don't have a gift, you will notice a look of disappointment on her face. Sure, mention your purchase, and you will notice the disappointment grow deeper.

WHAT TO DO WHEN THE RULE IS BROKEN: CHALK IT UP TO A LEARNING EXPERIENCE. GO BUY ANOTHER GIFT. IT'S YOUR ONLY WAY OUT.

Rule #14

WHEN A MAN BUYS SOMETHING THAT IS NOT A JOINT PURCHASE DECISION, YOU HAVE JUST GIVEN YOUR WIFE PERMISSION TO SPEND AT LEAST DOUBLE THAT AMOUNT.

Rule Application

If you are out and find something that the household needs, and buy it, you have just opened the door for your wife. See Rule #15 for why this is seen as a gift for yourself.

Your wife knows that you want to overindulge her to make her feel special. Therefore, seeing you have bought something for yourself, the logical conclusion is that you want her to buy something for herself of greater value. Twice the value is a good ballpark.

WHAT TO DO WHEN THE RULE IS BROKEN: FIRST, NEVER BUY ANYTHING OF VALUE WITHOUT FIRST CONSULTING WITH YOUR WIFE. AN "UNAUTHORIZED" PURCHASE SWINGS THE DOOR WIDE OPEN. SECOND, SELL HARD THAT THE PURCHASE IS FOR THE BENEFIT OF THE HOUSEHOLD. WHILE THIS USUALLY DOESN'T WORK, IT'S WORTH A SHOT. THIRD, BUY YOUR WIFE A SMALL GIFT WHILE YOU ARE OUT. THIS CAN OFTEN ELIMINATE THE NEED FOR HER TO GO OUT AND MAKE A PURCHASE TO EVEN THE SCORE.

Rule #15

When buying something for the household that can be shared, it will be considered your purchase.

Rule Application

The logic here is that whatever you purchase is yours, the family just gets the benefit of sharing it with you. Similar to Rule #15, only things that can only be used by your wife are considered her purchases. Everything else is yours.

WHAT TO DO WHEN THE RULE IS BROKEN: THERE IS NO DISCUSSION. THIS IS JUST THE WAY IT IS.

Rule #16

Outside of special occasions, a small gift for your wife counts the same as a large gift.

Rule Application

Special occasions require special gifts. Outside of those times, you will want to buy your wife gifts to surprise her or to let her know how special she is.

Most men make the mistake of not buying special gifts often because of the cost. They apply "man thinking." Man thinking is that the size of the gift is relative to your expression of love. Nothing could be further from the truth.

Your wife looks at special gifts as an act of communication. Just like the words, "I love you," speak volumes, a small gift has a great impact. It tells your wife that she encompasses all of your thoughts, large and small. So forget about cost, and pick up small, but significant, gifts along the way. It will do both of you good.

WHAT TO DO WHEN THE RULE IS BROKEN: IF YOU HAVE BEEN BUYING LARGE GIFTS, SCALE DOWN. IF YOU HAVEN'T BEEN BUYING ANY SPECIAL GIFTS, GET STARTED.

Rule #17

IF YOUR WIFE BUYS YOU A GIFT
THAT YOU DON'T CARE FOR, MAKE
A   STRONG   APPEARANCE   OF
APPRECIATION.

Rule Application

Particularly early in your marriage, while you are getting to know each other, you may receive a gift that doesn't work for you. Perhaps it is a jacket that would have looked good if "Miami Vice" was still in vogue. Or it could be some cologne that you wouldn't wear. Regardless, any show of rejection could be fatal.

If you reject a gift from your wife, she may take it as a personal rejection. Yes, I know that isn't how you meant it, but that doesn't matter. Accept the gift knowing that your wife bought it for you out of her love for you. See the love, not the gift. After wearing or using the gift for a good length of time, you may subtly hint on what you would like the next time, but not before a long time has passed.

WHAT TO DO WHEN THE RULE IS BROKEN: THERE ARE VARIOUS WAYS TO BREAK THIS RULE. YOU CAN OUT-RIGHT SAY THAT YOU DON'T LIKE IT (POOR CHOICE). YOU CAN SUGGEST THAT NEXT TIME, YOU WOULD LIKE SOME INPUT (STILL NOT GOOD, BUT BETTER THAN THE PREVIOUS ONE). OR YOU COULD JUST NOT USE OR WEAR IT. IN ALL CASES, YOUR WIFE WILL NOTE THE REJECTION.

The only way out of this one is to wear or use the gift. Do it as an act of love, for that is how the gift was given.

Rule #18

ON ROMANTIC HOLIDAYS, DON'T
INCLUDE, "WHAT'S FOR DINNER?"
IN YOUR SALUTATION.

Rule Application

"Happy Valentine's Day, what's for dinner?" While you may not see anything wrong with this phrase, you wife does. It places your personal desires above your appreciation for her, (which are your real needs). She wants to be appreciated every day, but especially on special holidays.

The first words out of your mouth when coming in the door should include all the reasons why you are delighted that you married your wife. (Some examples of these have been included in this book for those of you who are having trouble with this.) Set the mood by telling your wife how much you love her and appreciate her, and then take her out to dinner.

WHAT TO DO WHEN THE RULE IS BROKEN: VERY QUICKLY "GOTCH YA," FOLLOWED BY, "WHAT WOULD YOU LIKE FOR DINNER?" MEANING THAT YOU WILL FIX THE DINNER FOR YOUR WIFE. FOR THOSE WHO ARE CULINARY CHALLENGED (WHERE FIXING DINNER IS MORE A PUNISHMENT FOR EVERYONE EATING), YOU CAN USE THE PHRASE, "WHERE WOULD YOU LIKE TO GO OUT TO DINNER?" REMEMBER THAT SPEED IN RECOVERY COUNTS.

Rule #19

IF YOUR CHILDREN ASK YOUR PERMISSION, AND YOU ASK THEM WHAT MAMA SAID, ASK MAMA ANYWAY, REGARDLESS OF WHAT THEY SAY.

When Mama Ain't Happy...

Rule Application

What were you thinking when you asked your children what your wife said? Did you think they would tell you if she said, "No?" Of course not. There are two possible answers you can receive from children here:

"Mama said to ask you." Beware; this is a set-up, either by your children or your wife. If your children are setting you up, your wife probably told them, "I don't think you should, but if your father says it's OK, then you can." This is your wife's soft "No" to your kids and expects you to back her up.

"We haven't asked her yet." They already know what Mama's going to say, and are trying to get you to take their side before she has a chance to have the final vote. Don't fall for this. You know the majority automatically goes with your wife's vote.

WHAT TO DO WHEN THE RULE IS BROKEN: REVOKE PERMISSION. GET MAMA IN THE CONVERSATION.

Rule #20

ALLOW YOUR WIFE TO TALK TWICE AS MUCH AS YOU. SHE KNOWS THAT YOU ONLY LISTEN TO HALF OF WHAT SHE SAYS.

Rule Application

The next time you get a chance, watch another couple having a conversation between themselves. Does it seem like the wife is talking twice as much as the husband? It's actually a scientific fact (like that will keep me out of trouble for saying this) that women say twice as much as men. Now look at the husband. Does he even appear to be listening?

Now that your chuckles have subsided, realize that the same thing is going on in your relationship. Still funny?

WHAT TO DO WHEN THE RULE IS BROKEN: WOMEN TALK TWICE AS MUCH BECAUSE MEN ONLY LISTEN TO HALF OF WHAT IS SAID TO THEM. BESIDES, WHAT WOMEN SAY IS OFTEN IMPORTANT, SO IT BEARS REPEATING. GO WITH THE FLOW.

Rule #21

ASK DIRECTIONS, EVEN IF YOU THINK YOU MAY BE ABLE TO FIND YOUR WAY.

Rule Application

Yes, it is an unfair generalization that men don't ask for directions. OK, maybe not unfair, but a generalization. This means that your wife is going to be sensitive to getting lost in the car and having you drive around and not stopping for directions.

If you are not sure, stop and ask. Sure it may be a blow to your ego, but the guy you are asking knows why you are asking—not because you want to, but because your wife wants you to. He understands.

There is a side benefit to making a habit of asking for directions. The next time that your wife is in a group of people complaining that men have a malfunctioning gene that doesn't allow them to ask for directions, she can state, "My husband asks for directions." The oohs and aahs of the crowd will give your wife great pride.

WHAT TO DO WHEN THE RULE IS BROKEN: TWO SITUATIONS MAY OCCUR. FIRST, YOU MAY BE IN THE MIDST OF FINDING YOUR WAY (YOU'RE NOT LOST, OF COURSE)—STOP IMMEDIATELY AND ASK FOR DIRECTIONS. SECOND, IF YOU DO MANAGE TO FIND YOUR WAY, DON'T GLOAT. IT WON'T WORK. YOU'RE JUST LUCKY (THIS TIME). IN BOTH CASES BEGIN YOUR NEXT TRIP BY ASKING FOR DIRECTIONS, AND STOPPING LIBERALLY ALONG THE WAY TO VERIFY YOUR POSITION. YOUR WIFE WILL BE PROUD.

Rule #22

READ THE INSTRUCTIONS, EVEN
IF YOU DON'T NEED TO.

Rule Application

Men, in their desire for adventure, tend to jump into projects without reading the instructions. Sure, there are some notable exceptions to this, but no one seems to notice them. You are noticed when you have placed the table leg on upside down, the handlebars backwards, or have more pieces left over than when you started.

Begin each project by reading the directions. Or at least pretend you are reading them (please make sure they aren't upside down). If things are working, refer again to the directions. Keep this up until it becomes a habit.

WHAT TO DO WHEN THE RULE IS BROKEN: SO NOW YOU ARE SITTING IN FRONT OF YOUR PROJECT, AND IT CLEARLY ISN'T WORKING. THE INSTRUCTIONS ARE STILL TUCKED NEATLY IN THEIR UNOPENED PLASTIC BAG. YOU HAVE NO CHOICE BUT TO OPEN THEM UP AND READ THEM. SURE, YOUR INSTINCT IS TO TRY TO FIX WHAT-EVER YOU ARE DOING WITHOUT READING THE INSTRUCTIONS. JUST REMEMBER THAT THAT IS WHAT GOT YOU HERE IN THE FIRST PLACE.

. . . Ain't Nobody Happy

Rule #23

ALWAYS ANTICIPATE YOUR WIFE'S NEEDS, UNLESS SHE DOESN'T WANT YOU TO.

Rule Application

Everyone likes for someone to anticipate their needs. It makes us feel special. That we have a special bond with someone where we speak without speaking.

That is, unless, your wife feels that you are getting smug about this. That you know her so well that you don't even have to think about it, you just "know." When this happens, watch out. Your wife is about to make your life unpredictable.

WHAT TO DO WHEN THE RULE IS BROKEN: BE FLEXIBLE—ALWAYS. IF YOU NOTICE YOU DON'T SEEM TO BE GETTING THINGS RIGHT, YOUR WIFE IS TESTING YOU TO MAKE SURE THAT YOU ARE PAYING ATTENTION.

Pay extra special attention during this time. Assume that you don't know what you know and roll with the punches. The extra attentiveness will do you both some good.

Rule #24

WHEN YOU HEAR YOUR WIFE SINGING HER OWN PRAISES, IT'S A GOOD INDICATION THAT YOU ARE NOT DOING IT ENOUGH.

Rule Application

Your wife can be very subtle. It's her way to see if you are paying attention. If you usually fail this test, listen more carefully.

Your wife needs encouragement. If you don't provide enough of it, she will provide her own. Of course, she would rather have you do it, so she is going to use this as a hint. Pick up the hint and make a concerted effort over the next several days, or even weeks, to praise your wife.

WHAT TO DO WHEN THE RULE IS BROKEN: SO YOU HAVE FINALLY NOTICED THAT YOU ARE MISSING THE MARK HERE (OR MORE LIKELY YOU HAVE BEEN TOLD SO BY YOUR WIFE). APOLOGIES ARE A GREAT PLACE TO START FOLLOWED BY A LONG LIST OF ALL OF THE THINGS YOU APPRECIATE ABOUT YOUR WIFE. THEN TAKE THIS LIST OUT DAILY AND SELECT A FEW ITEMS TO PRAISE YOUR WIFE FOR. YOU WILL NOTICE A BIG CHANGE IN THE MOOD OF YOUR HOUSEHOLD.

. . . Ain't Nobody Happy

Rule #25

WHEN YOUR WIFE SAYS, "YOU WILL BE SORRY IF YOU…" DON'T INTERPRET THIS AS A VEILED WARNING; TAKE IT AS A PROMISE.

Rule Application

Women send some very clear signals sometimes. Sometimes, we men are just too thick to get it. When your wife says, "You'll be sorry," she means it. In fact, she is already thinking of ways to make you miserable for pursuing your plan. Take heed.

WHAT TO DO WHEN THE RULE IS BROKEN: OF ANYONE I KNOW I AM THE WORST IN HEEDING THIS ADVICE. I DON'T KNOW WHAT COMES OVER ME. MY WIFE WARNS ME, I HEAR THE WORDS, I UNDERSTAND THE MESSAGE, AND I KNOW WHAT IS GOING TO HAPPEN. YET, I SEEM TO BE COMPELLED BY SOME INVISIBLE FORCE TO CONTINUE ON. IT IS ALWAYS A MISTAKE.

The only way I have found to get out of this is to acknowledge the errors of my ways, and then work hard to treat my wife special for a long time. If anyone has anything else that works, I am all ears. I will probably place myself in this situation again.

Rule #26

YOUR WIFE WILL ALWAYS HEAR
WHAT YOU SAY (WHETHER SHE IS
THERE OR NOT), SO BE FLATTERING
AND POSITIVE.

Rule Application

How many men have said something about their wives only to have it come back to her. It doesn't have to be bad to create problems for you, just misunderstood.

Knowing this, whatever you say outside of your wife's presence should be more flattering and kind than if she were there. Given that anything that can be misinterpreted will (Murphy's Law), make sure that it is so nice, that it can only be taken that way.

WHAT TO DO WHEN THE RULE IS BROKEN: IF YOU STEP IN IT, PLAY THE RHYME AND/OR SIMILE GAME. FOR EXAMPLE, YOUR WIFE MAY BE TOLD THAT YOU SAID, "MY WIFE MAY BE PUTTING ON SOME WEIGHT." YOU WOULD SAY, "NO. WHAT I SAID WAS, 'I WANT TO SEE YOU SO BAD, I CAN'T WAIT.'" IF YOUR WIFE WAS TOLD YOU SAID, "DINNER LAST NIGHT WAS CRAPPY." YOU SAY, "NO. I SAID THAT DINNER WAS SO GOOD THAT I LEFT THE TABLE HAPPY."

While your wife won't fall for this, she knows, and now you know, you won't make this mistake again. Hopefully.

Rule #27

Even in a pair of dirty jeans,
see the beauty of your wife.

Rule Application

When you were first dating your wife, she was beautiful regardless of what she looked like because you saw the beauty inside of her. That is where her real beauty lies. Women like to be reminded of this, especially when they may not look their best on the outside. It is during these times, reminding your wife of her beauty reminds her of how lovely she really is.

WHAT TO DO WHEN THE RULE IS BROKEN: SO YOU JUST TOLD YOUR WIFE TO GO CHANGE BEFORE YOU GO OUT TO THE STORE. MISTAKE—BIG MISTAKE. THIS IS WHERE SPIN CONTROL COMES IN HANDY.

What you need to tell your wife is that you want everyone to know how beautiful she really is. But you know how shallow people are today, they only look at the outside. They don't have the advantage of knowing the real woman she is. You just want other people to see what you see. And then promise yourself that you won't make this mistake again.

Rule #28

WHEN REFERRING TO YOUR WIFE'S AGE, USE THE FOLLOWING:

IF YOUR WIFE IS YOUNGER, THE TERM TO USE IS "MUCH YOUNGER."

IF YOUR WIFE IS YOUR AGE, USE "YOUNGER."

IF YOUR WIFE IS OLDER, SHE IS "MY AGE."

When Mama Ain't Happy . . .

Rule Application

Your wife's age, in her mind, is relative to yours. Therefore, throughout your marriage, how young she feels is how old she feels relative to you.

I have found (through unfortunate experience) that most women don't like you to think that they look their age, or worse, older. Therefore, always subtract a few years from your wife's age relative to yours. It will keep her feeling young.

WHAT TO DO WHEN THE RULE IS BROKEN: THIS IS VERY DIFFICULT TO GET OUT OF, IF YOU MAKE A MISTAKE. IT'S BAD ENOUGH WHEN YOU ACCURATELY DESCRIBE YOUR WIFE'S AGE, WORSE WHEN YOU MAKE HER OLDER (USUALLY DONE WHEN YOU ARE TRYING TO MAKE YOUR-SELF LOOK YOUNGER) THAN SHE IS.

My best advice is first, to duck. Then see the Rule of Two (Rule #2, of course).

Rule #29

A FEW GRAY HAIRS ON YOUR WIFE SHOULD BE CONSIDERED INVISIBLE. ANY MORE THAN THAT ARE "NATURAL HIGHLIGHTS."

When Mama Ain't Happy . . .

Rule Application

No one likes getting gray hair. Some people don't mind it, but nobody likes it. Therefore, any reference to gray hair should be positive.

Chances are, you probably didn't see any gray hair on your wife until she pointed it out to you (you didn't notice her last hairdo, so why would you notice this?). So, if she shows you her gray hair take an extra long time looking for it and only notice it after her repeated attempts to show it to you. When she has enough gray that you can't ignore it, change the color from gray to natural highlights. It will make her less conscious of the gray, and you happier.

WHAT TO DO WHEN THE RULE IS BROKEN: FIRST OF ALL, YOU MUST UNDERSTAND THAT YOU ARE THE REASON FOR YOUR WIFE'S GRAY HAIR. SO POINTING IT OUT ONLY BRINGS ATTENTION TO YOU.

If you do make the mistake of pointing out the gray hair, tell your wife how sophisticated and sensual she looks with it. Nobody can wear gray hair and make it a fashion statement like your wife.

Rule #30

WHEN ALL ELSE FAILS, THROW YOURSELF AT THE MERCY OF YOUR WIFE.

When Mama Ain't Happy . . .

Rule Application

OK, so you blew it really bad. You broke several rules within the span of a few minutes (I've seen it happen, and it's not a pretty sight). Things are so bad, that it looks like there is no way out. Get out your knee pads and grovel. Throw yourself on the mercy of the court.

WHAT TO DO WHEN THE RULE IS BROKEN: THE COMMON MISTAKE MEN MAKE HERE IS UNDERESTIMATING THE DAMAGE. IT'S LIKE LOOKING AT SOMEONE WHO HAS JUST LOST A LIMB, AND TELLING THEM IT'S ONLY A SCRATCH. MAKE AN ACCURATE ASSESSMENT. FACE YOUR PROBLEMS HEAD ON.

No matter how long you hold out, no matter how much punishment you endure, you are going to have to plead for mercy. There is no other way out.

Rule #31

WHEN PLANNING TO DO HOME PROJECTS, PLAN ON DOING ALL OF THE WORK YOURSELF, UNLESS YOUR WIFE DOESN'T WANT YOU TO.

Rule Application

Your wife doesn't really want to participate in the home project, she just wants to see it completed. The exception to this is when your wife has serious doubts about your capabilities with the project. In that case, she will become very involved to make sure you don't burn the house down.

WHAT TO DO WHEN THE RULE IS BROKEN: THERE ARE TWO WAYS TO BREAK THE RULE. THE FIRST, AND LESS SERIOUS, IS TO TRY TO GET YOUR WIFE INVOLVED WHEN SHE HAS NO INTEREST IN THE PROJECT. HERE, YOU WILL HAVE TO ENDURE A LACK OF INTEREST—KIND OF LIKE WHEN YOU WATCH A FOOTBALL GAME. IF YOU ARE LUCKY, AS I HAVE BEEN, YOUR WIFE WILL PARTICIPATE WITH YOU TO SATISFY YOUR DESIRE TO HAVE HER PARTICIPATE. THIS HOWEVER, COMES AT A PRICE. YOU WILL BE EXPECTED TO PARTICIPATE IN ONE OF HER PROJECTS THAT YOU HAVE NO INTEREST.

The more serious of the two, is to forget to allow your wife to participate when she wants to. She will interpret her exclusion as a total disregard of your family's safety and welfare on your part. (And she may be right.) Bring her in on the project as soon as you realize this and be prepared to redo anything you have done. If you have completed the project, be prepared to bring in professional help to have them inspect your project.

Rule #32

YOUR WIFE NEVER LOOKS FAT.

Not a Personal Story:
Wife: Do I look fat?
Husband: Do I look crazy?
(This may be perhaps the only proper answer to this question.)

Rule Application

Hint: It's those darn clothes that keep shrinking and won't fit right anymore.

WHAT TO DO WHEN THE RULE IS BROKEN: I CAN'T GIVE YOU ANY FIRST HAND EXPERIENCE ON THIS, SINCE MY WIFE HAS BEEN THIN SINCE THE DAY WE MET UP TO NOW (SEE HOW WELL I HAVE LEARNED THESE RULES?).

Rule #33

REMEMBER THAT YOUR GREATEST ACHIEVEMENTS ARE ALWAYS DUE TO YOUR WIFE'S SUPPORT.

Rule Application

Remember what you were like before you met your wife? This in itself should prove this point.

I have heard it said that behind every great man are great women and a surprised mother-in-law. We should at least consider the first point here to be true.

WHAT TO DO WHEN THE RULE IS BROKEN: EVERY MAN HAS MADE THE MISTAKE OF TAKING THE CREDIT FOR HIS ACCOMPLISHMENTS. THAT'S OK, BUT YOU HAVE TO SHARE THE LIMELIGHT WITH YOUR WIFE.

Here's the rule: For every time you take the credit alone. You have to reject the credit and give it to your wife—twice. When the balance sheet is even, abide by Rule #18.

Rule #34

YOUR RELATIONSHIP WITH YOUR
WIFE TAKES PRECEDENCE OVER
YOUR RELATIONSHIP WITH YOUR
CHILDREN.

Rule Application

You will live with your wife for the rest of your life. Your children will leave home some day (you hope). This is one of the best pieces of advice my mother-in-law gave me. It helped me understand how I should prioritize my relationships.

When you come home from work, everyone wants your attention. By their nature, children are more aggressive at getting attention, so it's easy to give them attention first to satisfy them, and then to spend time with your wife. However, the best lesson you can give your children for their future is that Mama comes first in everything, including attention. Your children will thank you for when they have households of their own.

WHAT TO DO WHEN THE RULE IS BROKEN: WE ALL LOVE OUR CHILDREN. IN REALITY, THOUGH, THEY JUST CAME ALONG AS A RESULT OF OUR RELATIONSHIP WITH OUR WIFE. AND WHEN THEY ARE GONE, IT IS GOING TO BE THE TWO OF YOU, AGAIN.

Make every effort to build a relationship that will be stronger after the children leave. Every time you break this rule, make amends quickly, and learn from that experience.

Rule #35

NEVER LET YOUR WIFE GO TO BED ANGRY WITH YOU. REMEMBER THAT SHE IS THE BENEFICIARY OF YOUR LIFE INSURANCE POLICY.

Rule Application

My friend, Brent Preece, educated me on this rule. Your wife has everything to gain from your untimely departure from this earth. Can you say, "Double indemnity?" Not only does she benefit, but she has unlimited access. "She wouldn't do that. She couldn't get away with it." Are you willing to bet your life on that?

In all seriousness, when someone goes to bed angry, that anger festers. Festering anger only grows larger and deeper. Don't you want to prevent that?

WHAT TO DO WHEN THE RULE IS BROKEN: FIRST, DO EVERYTHING IN YOUR POWER TO RESOLVE YOUR DIFFERENCES BEFORE YOU BOTH GO TO BED. EVEN IF IT TAKES ALL NIGHT. IT'S WORTH THE EFFORT.

If somehow you miss this opportunity, try to resolve the situation first thing in the morning, or as soon as possible. If you don't, her day will be ruined, and yours too. Remember, "When Mama ain't happy, ain't nobody happy."

Rule #36

NEVER TELL YOUR WIFE THAT SHE
REMINDS YOU OF YOUR MOTHER.

When Mama Ain't Happy . . .

Rule Application

No matter how flattering this comment is meant to be, it will never be taken as a compliment. Most men love their mothers. I know I do. But my relationship with my mother is very different than my relationship with my wife.

My mother is someone who took care of me, directed me and cleaned up after me (at least up to an age). My wife doesn't want to be thought of in that way. She wants to be a partner, a friend, someone I do for. Our relationship with our mothers are never quite thought of in that way. To put your wife in that role takes her down a peg.

WHAT TO DO WHEN THE RULE IS BROKEN: THE ONLY THING YOU CAN DO AT THIS POINT IS TO SELL HARD. TELL YOUR WIFE THAT YOU ONLY MEANT THIS IN THE MOST POSITIVE SENSE: SHE IS CARING AND GIVING, A SUPERWOMEN. (THEN SELL HARDER.)

Then remind your wife that she is even more. She is a confident, a friend, a lover, someone you want spend your life with. Remind her that you left your mother to spend your life with her. That should say it all.

Rule #37

NEVER USE THE WORD "FUN" WHEN ON A BUSINESS TRIP.

Personal Story: During a business trip, the company hosting the event rented a theme park for the evening for attendees of the conference. It happened to be one of my favorite theme parks. In a favorite theme park, without the lines and crowds, without having to pay, having nearly unlimited time, how could I not have fun?

When I got back to my hotel room, as every night I called home to talk to my wife. When asked how I liked the evening, the word "fun" slipped out. Dead silence. I guess the evening dining on hot dogs with three small children created too stark a contrast in our evenings. It is a lesson that I will never forget.

Rule Application

Business trips aren't supposed to be fun. If you remember not to whistle while you pack, you can ruin it all by using the word fun inappropriately in a conversation. It's not that your wife doesn't want you to have fun. Sure she does. She just doesn't want to be reminded that you are having fun without her.

Always remember to remind your wife that, no matter where you are, you wish she was there with you. Her company makes any trip better.

WHAT TO DO WHEN THE RULE IS BROKEN: FIRST, TRY TO RECOVER QUICKLY. IF YOU TELL YOUR WIFE, "WE WENT OUT LAST NIGHT AND SAW THE CITY. YEAH, IT WAS FUN." TRY TO ADD ON, "BUT NOT AS FUN AS IF YOU WERE HERE. NOW THAT I THINK ABOUT IT, I NEVER HAVE AS MUCH FUN AS WHEN I AM WITH YOU."

Remember to use the word "miserable" liberally during the rest of your trip.

Rule #38

WHEN PEOPLE COMPLIMENT YOU ABOUT YOUR CHILDREN, ATTRIBUTE THOSE GOOD GRACES TO YOUR WIFE.

Rule Application

Think about how you acted before you met your wife. Now think about your life now. Dramatic improvement! You married your wife, at least in part, because of her good graces. It's those good graces that people see in your children. You may have learned them from your wife, but she is the source. Give credit where credit is due.

WHAT TO DO WHEN THE RULE IS BROKEN: FIRST, IF YOU TAKE CREDIT, NO ONE WILL BELIEVE YOU. SO IF YOU CATCH YOURSELF QUICKLY, "JUST KIDDING," WORKS FINE. THEN LAUNCH INTO HOW HAPPY YOU ARE THAT YOU MARRIED YOUR WIFE AND HOW LUCKY YOUR KIDS ARE TO HAVE PICKED UP HER HABITS RATHER THAN YOURS.

If, for some reason, you fail to make this recovery, the rule of two goes into effect. The rule of two is that your redemption comes only after you have gone out of you way to give your wife credit twice as many times as you took credit. Remember, you have to go out of your way to create the situation to give your wife credit. If the opportunity presents itself, it doesn't count in the rule of two.

Rule #39
(Corollary to Rule #38)

IF PEOPLE COMPLAIN ABOUT YOUR CHILDREN, ATTRIBUTE THOSE BAD GRACES TO YOURSELF.

When Mama Ain't Happy . . .

Rule Application

The corollary to Rule #38. Given that your children received all the good graces from your wife, they couldn't have received the bad ones from her too. That leaves you.

Remember all the bad things that you did when you were a kid? Somehow, they have seeped into your kid's brain to wreak havoc in your life. You have received, what my father calls the Irish blessing, "May your children be to you what you were to me." Scary thought.

WHAT TO DO WHEN THE RULE IS BROKEN: IF YOU ATTRIBUTED ANY BAD GRACES TO YOUR WIFE, THE RULE OF TWO (RULE #2) GOES INTO EFFECT.

Rule #40

REMEMBER TO THANK YOUR IN-
LAWS FOR RAISING SUCH A
WONDERFUL DAUGHTER.

Rule Application

Face it. When you met your wife, her parents instilled the characteristics that attracted you to her. You had nothing to do with it. And as you continue in your marriage, much of her perspective comes from what her parents taught her.

Give credit where credit is due. Your in-laws will appreciate your insight and wisdom.

WHAT TO DO WHEN THE RULE IS BROKEN: NEVER, UNDER ANY CIRCUMSTANCES, TAKE CREDIT FOR THE GOOD ATTRIBUTES OF YOUR WIFE. NOT ONLY IS IT NOT TRUE, IT WILL BE CONSIDERED AN INSULT.

If you make this unconscionable error, apply the rule of two (Rule #2) to your in-laws. You will be glad that you did.

Rule #41

REMEMBER THAT ALL THAT YOU
HAVE, YOU SHARE, UNLESS IT'S
HERS.

Rule Application

I was shocked when I learned this rule from a friend. This is more of a "Southern" rule. Most wives, at least tactically, like the concept.

Here is the concept. If both of you work, the man's paycheck goes to paying the bills (even if you don't work, this is generally held to be true). The woman's paycheck becomes her own to do with what she wants. It's her "play" money.

WHAT TO DO WHEN THE RULE IS BROKEN: FRANKLY, I DON'T GET THIS RULE. PERHAPS THAT IS BECAUSE THIS RULE NEVER CAME INTO MY HOUSE. MY WIFE ALWAYS INCLUDED HER PAYCHECK IN WITH MINE—LUCKY GUY THAT I AM.

This is probably the only rule in this book that I would say, if the rule is broken, celebrate (quietly, of course). Count your blessings.

Rule #42

LET YOUR WIFE START GETTING
DRESSED FIRST. IT'S YOUR JOB
TO COORDINATE YOUR CLOTHES
WITH HERS.

Rule Application

Women like to be coordinated with their husbands when they dress well. Clashing does not go well in their book. In fact, most won't tolerate it.

So let her get dressed first. When it is time for you to get dressed, double check with your wife that she approves of what you have picked out (safety precaution).

Don't try to short cut this by asking your wife what you should wear before she gets dressed. It won't work. Your wife will likely take the prerogative to change her mind.

WHAT TO DO WHEN THE RULE IS BROKEN: BE PREPARED TO CHANGE.

If you get dressed first, chances are you have selected something that will clash. Now this isn't totally your fault. Your choice has actually motivated your wife to select something that will clash. (Don't ask me to explain this, it just happens this way.)

As you stand there (not noticing that your clothes aren't coordinated), your wife will look at you like, "You aren't wearing that, are you?" You know the look. Don't ask for an explanation, just change.

Rule #43

WHEN DISCUSSING COLORS, SCENTS OR TEXTURES, YOUR WIFE IS MORE PRECISE THAN YOU ARE.

Rule Application

When I pick up a sheet of paper and call it pink, my wife reminds me it is mauve. "No, that's not purple, its lavender." "Definitely not red, rose."

Women tend to have a more precise sense of color, scents and textures. If your wife draws the distinction, trust her, she's right.

WHAT TO DO WHEN THE RULE IS BROKEN: GO AHEAD AND ARGUE WITH YOUR WIFE ABOUT THESE THINGS. SHE KNOWS THAT SHE IS RIGHT, (WHICH MAKES YOU WRONG). ARGUING WITH HER WON'T CHANGE ANYTHING. IT ONLY REINFORCES WHAT SHE KNOWS. SHE IS BETTER AT IDENTIFYING COLORS, SCENTS AND TEXTURES THAN YOU ARE. ACQUIESCE, AND INCREASE YOUR VOCABULARY. SOME DAY, YOUR WIFE MAY REFER TO YOU AS A "RENAISSANCE MAN."

Rule #44

WHEN DECORATING YOUR HOME,
THE BEST YOU CAN HOPE FOR IS
TO HAVE INPUT INTO ONE ROOM.

I lived on my own for some time before I met Kris. I owned my own home and had my way of doing things. When we were married, I assumed that we would make joint decisions.

After we were married, we moved and purchased a new home. We began redecorating the living room, which Kris wanted in pink. My response was, "No way."

By the time the wallpaper, Oriental rug, and paint were picked out, the room was pink! Although I tried to influence the choices, Kris got her way. While she still refers to those colors as "champagne," to me it is still pink.

Rule Application

Our homes are decorated by our wives and have their touch, their flair, and their personality.

Most women, though, will allow men one room. It may be a TV room, a home bar, a game room, but most likely will be the garage. In these places the men can decorate things the way they want. Leather, moose heads, beer signs abound. Your wife lets you do this to serve as a reminder why you were only given one room and not the whole house. When was the last time visitors complimented you on your room?

WHAT TO DO WHEN THE RULE IS BROKEN: NO MATTER HOW LONG AND HARD YOU ARGUE, YOUR WIFE WILL NEVER GIVE IN. TO LIVE IN EMPTY ROOMS IS BETTER THAN BEING SURROUNDED BY THE CARCASSES OF DEAD ANIMALS, IS HER LOGIC. AND SHE'S RIGHT. PEOPLE COMPLIMENT YOUR WIFE ON HER DECORATING, NOT BECAUSE THEY ARE BEING NICE, BUT BECAUSE IT'S TRUE. THEY ARE BEING NICE WHEN THEY DON'T COMMENT ON YOUR ROOM.

Rule #45

WHEN DECIDING ON A HOUSE TO BUY, CHOOSE THE ONE YOUR WIFE LIKES.

Personal Story: When we moved to Raleigh, North Carolina a few years ago, my objective was to buy a house for the same price we sold our house for in Austin, Texas. We looked around at a number of houses and found a nice house that met our criteria. We put a bid on the house and drove back to the hotel to relax for the evening.

On the drive back to the hotel, I noticed that Kris was distant (a clear sign that I broke a rule—now I just had to figure out which one). After prodding for several minutes (I don't mind asking for the answer), Kris explained that she hoped we could by a different house. Of course the house she liked was considerably more money than we had planned on spending.

Fortunately, the bid on "my" house was rejected and we bought "her" house. Result? Mama was happy!

Rule Application

To men, a home is a place to live. To women, home is where lives are created and developed, and memories live. The wrong house creates the wrong memories. The right house creates a brighter future—for you!

WHAT TO DO WHEN THE RULE IS BROKEN: SELL THE HOUSE. IT IS THE ONLY WAY OUT. START AGAIN—THIS TIME, ACCORDING TO THE RULES.

Rule #46

VACATION FOR YOUR WIFE MEANS
NO CHILDREN.

When Mama Ain't Happy . . .

Rule Application

Women like romantic getaways. Children and romance are mutually exclusive.

WHAT TO DO WHEN THE RULE IS BROKEN: TAKING A VACATION WITH YOUR KIDS DOESN'T COUNT, EVEN IF IT IS TO THE PLACE OF YOUR WIFE'S CHOOSING. A WEEKEND AT A NICE HOTEL, VISITING A PLACE SHE HAS TALKED ABOUT, OR EVEN TAKING A DAY ALONE TOGETHER COUNTS, AS LONG AS IT IS WITHOUT THE KIDS. TRY TO DO THIS AT LEAST ONCE EVERY YEAR.

Rule #47

TELL YOUR WIFE THAT YOU LOVE
HER AT LEAST THREE TIMES EACH
DAY. KEEP A TALLY SHEET IN
YOUR POCKET, IF NECESSARY.

Rule Application

My wife claims that this number is more like twenty. I have set the minimum. It's kind of like Vitamin C for your wife. There is a minimum dosage, but more doesn't hurt. (And it clears your system every day, so you need to take it daily!)

For whatever the reason, most women want to hear (and then demonstrate) how much they are loved. Men don't need to hear it as much, but this is not for you; it is for her.

I recommend (at minimum) that you tell your wife in the morning before you go to work. Give her a call during the day to tell her again. Remember to tell her before you go to bed. Adding words to tell her why you love her provide bonus points.

What amazes me is that each time you tell your wife, her expression will be as though she hasn't heard it in a while. It's that look of refreshment, a look of pleasure. Make your wife happy, and tell her that you love her.

WHAT TO DO WHEN THE RULE IS BROKEN: IF YOU HAVEN'T BEEN DOING THIS, DOUBLE UP TO MAKE UP FOR LOST TIME. KEEP ON GOING WITH AT LEAST SIX "I LOVE YOU'S," PER DAY UNTIL YOU HAVE CAUGHT UP. BY THAT TIME, YOU WILL BE SO USED TO IT THAT IT WILL BECOME A NATURAL PART OF YOUR DAY.

Rule #48

WHEN ORDERING YOUR MEAL,
ORDER FOOD THAT YOUR WIFE
WILL ENJOY. IT WILL MAKE THE
MEAL MORE ENJOYABLE.

Rule Application

My wife doesn't share food in a restaurant often. But I know she has her eye on what is on my plate.

Men are territorial, women are communal. Husbands don't want to share. Wives enjoy the experience more when they can share with what you have. They also expect you to share with what's on their plate. (OK guys, fight the feeling. You don't need to share, but she wants you to.)

WHAT TO DO WHEN THE RULE IS BROKEN: FIRST, DON'T SAY, "HEY IF YOU WANTED SOMETHING ELSE, YOU SHOULD HAVE ORDERED IT." (VERY INSENSITIVE.) JUST FOLLOW THESE THREE SIMPLE STEPS:

APOLOGIZE.

OFFER TO SELECT SOMETHING FOR DESERT THAT YOU CAN SHARE.

REMEMBER THIS THE NEXT TIME YOU GO OUT TO EAT.

Rule #49

WHEN YOUR WIFE IS SETTING
YOU UP, YOU CAN'T ACT LIKE YOU
KNOW YOU ARE BEING SET UP.

Rule Application

It's happened to us all. We can see it coming. We are being set up. You know the signs. "Do you want some company to go to the auto parts store?" "Would you like me to go to the hardware store with you?" You know that there is a clothing store nearby and that you are being asked to come along to give your opinion on a purchase.

There is no way out. If you tell your wife that you know what she is up to, you will hurt her feelings. So just go along with it. You may even enjoy yourself.

WHAT TO DO WHEN THE RULE IS BROKEN: WHEN YOU UNCOVER THE PLOT, YOU WILL SEE A FACE RIDDLED WITH DISAPPOINTMENT. QUICKLY SAY, "BUT THAT'S GOOD. I WAS HOPING WE COULD GO TO THE CLOTHING STORE SOMETIME TODAY. THIS IS A GREAT OPPORTUNITY!" WHETHER YOUR WIFE BELIEVES YOU OR NOT, YOU HAVE PUT DOWN THE WELCOME MAT TO DO WHAT SHE WAS PLANNING. THAT SMILE WILL COME BACK ON HER BEAUTIFUL FACE.

Rule #50

WHEN NEWLY MARRIED, YOU WILL BE ASKED BY YOUR FRIENDS HOW YOU LIKE BEING MARRIED. THE BEST RESPONSE TO THIS IS, "IF I HAD KNOWN MARRIAGE WAS GOING TO BE THIS GOOD, I WOULD HAVE MARRIED MY WIFE MUCH EARLIER."

Rule Application

I was twenty-eight when we were married. After waiting this long, my friends were curious about how I was doing. My honest response was, "If I had known marriage was going to be this good, I would have married Kris much earlier."

What I noticed as I said this was that Kris' countenance brightened. As quick as I am, I realized that this was an affirmation to her on how much I loved and cared for her.

WHAT TO DO WHEN THE RULE IS BROKEN: LOOK, YOU ARE GOING TO BE WITH THIS WOMAN FOR THE REST OF YOUR LIFE. GET WITH THE PROGRAM.

If you are having difficulty with this, I would recommend practicing in front of the mirror. The right amount of enthusiasm is very important. Too little enthusiasm and you are not believable. Too much enthusiasm and you seem insincere. When you reach a point that you are comfortable with this in front of a mirror, try it out on some friends (preferably married friends so that you can get good feedback). Once you have mastered it, you can try it in public.

Rule #51

ALWAYS COMPLIMENT YOUR WIFE'S COOKING. IT WILL SAVE YOU FROM GOING HUNGRY.

Rule Application

Because Kris works keeping our house going, she does the cooking. I am a good cook, and help out as often as I can, but I am very fortunate that my wife is an excellent cook. I always try to compliment her on her cooking. It helps her see how appreciative I am of her extraordinary efforts.

WHAT TO DO WHEN THE RULE IS BROKEN: IF YOU BREAK THIS RULE, DO THE COOKING YOURSELF FOR A TIME. THIS WILL REMIND YOU WHAT YOUR BACHELOR DAYS WERE LIKE. MCDONALD'S WILL HAVE A FINE DINING RING TO IT AFTER A FEW DAYS. AFTER THIS, APOLOGIZE, PREFERABLY ON YOUR KNEES.

Rule #52

REMEMBER THAT MARRIAGE IS NOT 50/50, IT'S 100/100.

Rule Application

The trouble is, when you try to meet someone half way, both people define half way differently. This difference creates more conflict than necessary. No one wants to go past "their" halfway point.

By defining marriage as a 100/100 proposition, you understand that you are expected to do everything you can for your wife. Half a job is not a good job. All out is the only way to go.

You will find that when you take on this attitude that your wife meets you more than halfway almost all of the time. Your halfway points weren't that far apart after all. You were missing this great treat by focusing on inches instead of years.

WHAT TO DO WHEN THE RULE IS BROKEN: TAKE ON A NEW ATTITUDE. GO FOR THE GUSTO, GO ALL THE WAY!

Warning

THESE RULES MAY CHANGE WITHOUT NOTICE, AT THE OPTION OF YOUR WIFE.

Rule Application

My father taught me this a long time ago. Except his rule was that whenever your wife discovered that you understood the rules, she would change them. I guess that was my Mom's application of the rule. I have made it a little broader to capture a few more households.

Your wife wants you to be able to anticipate her needs, but she doesn't want to be predictable. Being predictable is equated with unappreciated. She knows this when you begin to do things by rote (like you're trying to check it off a list rather than for her). There is a world of difference between the two.

WHAT TO DO WHEN THE RULE IS BROKEN: THERE ARE TWO WAYS IN WHICH THIS RULE IS USUALLY BROKEN. THE FIRST WAY IS WHEN YOUR WIFE CHANGES THE RULES, BUT YOU INSIST THAT YOU KNOW WHAT THE RULE IS. THE FACT THAT YOU ARE SO CONFIDENT YOU KNOW THE RULE MAY BE THE VERY REASON FOR THE CHANGE. DON'T TRY TO ARGUE YOUR POINT. IT'S LIKE TRYING TO ARGUE THAT GRAVITY DOESN'T EXIST.

The second way you can break the rule is to do it by rote, as mentioned above. Rote is that smug way that we men act when we think we have the system beat. You may not think you are doing that, but your smugness gives off a fragrance every woman can smell. Get out of that mindset. Otherwise, your wife has no choice but to change the rule(s) to get your attention.

Conclusion

TEACH YOUR CHILDREN THESE
RULES FROM BIRTH.

Rule Application

Think about this. When you were married, you were how old? And you didn't even know these rules existed! Make it easy on your children, especially your sons, and teach them these rules before they can even talk. Hey, kids are pretty smart these days. They'll catch on quickly.

WHAT TO DO WHEN THE RULE IS BROKEN: THERE REALLY ISN'T ANYTHING AWFUL ABOUT NOT TEACHING YOUR CHILDREN ABOUT THE RULES. IT WILL JUST MAKE YOUR LIFE MORE DIFFICULT. YOU SEE, MAMA'S HAPPINESS IS EVERYBODY'S JOB. IF THE KIDS DON'T KNOW WHAT TO DO, THEY ARE GOING TO MAKE MAMA UNHAPPY. AND YOU KNOW WHAT THIS MEANS.

Build a spirit of cooperation with your children. It will make everyone's life easier.

Epilogue

I've now done all that I can to help you have a happy household. I have given you my years of experience. I have explained things to you in a simple and logical way. I have even told you how to undo the trouble you have wrought on yourself. What more can I do?

Now its your turn. Study these rules. Commit them to memory (the next chapter is a summary list of the rules to help you on this). You may even want to make laminated cards to carry in your wallet. The better you know them, and use them, the better off you will be.

Are these a complete list of rules? Absolutely not. An unwritten rule is that your wife can make up any rule at any time for any reason—without notice. It's up to you to identify and define these rules. Once you learn to live by the core set of rules laid out here, it will be easy for you to recognize new rules. Write them down, too. Commit them to memory. You get the idea.

You also have an obligation to others in the male race. If you notice someone in the brotherhood who obviously doesn't know that there are rules (remember that you were there once, too) take some time out and explain to him the way this works. Start with Rule #1, "When Mama ain't happy, ain't nobody happy." Then go from there. Every kindness that you show to others will be shown to you. Besides, he who teaches learns twice.

I trust that you have enjoyed your time reading this book. I certainly enjoyed writing it. And remember the battle cry:

"MMH" (Make Mama Happy)

MMH (Make Mama Happy) Test
(How well have you learned the rules?)

Check the most appropriate answers and then check and score your answers at the end of this chapter. You get one point for each right answer. Wrong answers can get you a score of 1 or negative 1, depending on how bad the answer (just like real life). Good luck!

1. The mood in my home is established by:

   A. The phases of the moon.
   B. The phases that my children are going through.
   C. Me.
   D. My wife.

2. When my wife gives me "that look" I should:

   A. Ignore her. She will go away.
   B. Beg and plead for forgiveness (even if I have no idea why I am getting the look).
   C. Just say, "No."
   D. Try to give her the look back.

3. When my wife asks me if she looks fat, the correct answer is:

   A. No more than when we were married.
   B. Yeah, but I wouldn't worry about it, because I will always love you.
   C. No way! You are a very sexy woman.
   D. Gee, I'm not quite sure how I am supposed to answer that.

4. It's my wife's birthday and I have forgotten to buy her a present. I should:

A. Spend whatever time and money necessary to get her an unforgettable gift.
B. Go home and tell her I thought it would be nice for us to go out shopping together to get her present.
C. Tell her I was planning on combining her birthday gift with the next holiday gift.
D. Don't worry about it. She'll have another birthday next year.

5. I have just purchased my wife an expensive dress. She has just asked to go out to a very nice restaurant. I should:

A. Have expected this and planned for it.
B. Try to convince her that fast food has become chic.
C. Tell her, "No way, not after what we spent on that dress!"
D. Stare at her in disbelief.

6. You and your wife have just had a major disagreement at 11 p.m. You should:

A. Forget about it and go to sleep.
B. Go to sleep in a set of medieval armor.
C. Get right with God before you go to sleep. His face may be the next face you see.
D. Get right with your wife right away. She may be counting her inheritance as you speak.

7. You notice that your favorite sweater has been missing for months. You suddenly come across it in your wife's closet. You should:

A. Go buy a new sweater realizing that this, too, may find the same fate.
B. Sneak it back into your closet.
C. Wear it boldly in front of your wife.
D. Instruct your wife to stay out of your stuff.

8. Your children (out of character) have just embarrassed you in a public place. You should:

   A. Walk away from them and act like you don't know to whom they belong.
   B. Take them to security and have them locked up until their parents come for them.
   C. Point to your wife and loudly say, "I told you that they take after your side of the family."
   D. Look at your children and say, "I used to behave like that when I was a child. I just hope you are lucky enough to marry someone like your Mom so that these bad genes can be flushed out of our gene pool."

9. You are at a company function that includes spouses. Your boss has just complimented you in front of a group of people on your latest project. You should say,

   A. "It is difficult being a modern husband, balancing work, family, and community activities, but I am able to handle it."
   B. "Thanks, boss. I am glad you appreciate my work."
   C. "My work group really deserves the credit."
   D. "Thank you. I appreciate the support. But I would also like to publicly thank my wife. For I find that every great accomplishment that I have made in my life could not have been done without her."

10. I'm trying to use the rules and they're not working because:

   A. I'm really not paying attention and I need to.
   B. My wife doesn't have rules.
   C. I was perfect before, and any changes make me less so.
   D. I don't think there are such things as rules in my household.

Answers to the Test

1. (a) 0 points
   (b) 0 points
   (c) -1 point
   (d) 1 point

2. (a) 0 points
   (b) 1 point
   (c) -1 point
   (d) 0 points

3. (a) -1 point
   (b) -1 point
   (c) 1 point
   (d) 0 points

4. (a) 1 point
   (b) 0 points
   (c) -1 point
   (d) -1 point

5. (a) 1 point
   (b) -1 point
   (c) -1 point
   (d) -1 point

6. (a) -1 point
   (b) 0 points
   (c) 0 points
   (d) 1 point

7. (a) 1 point
   (b) 0 points
   (c) 0 points
   (d) -1 point

8. (a)   0 points
   (b)   0 points
   (c) -1 point
   (d)   1 point

9. (a) -1 point
   (b)   0 points
   (c)   0 points
   (d)   1 point

10.(a)   1 point
   (b) -1 point
   (c) -1 point
   (d) -1 point

Score 10: Mama is happy! Consider starting a "Big Husband" program in your community to help those less fortunate than yourself.

Score 8–9: Hey, not bad! You are in the top quartile of your class.

Score 6–7: You may want to brush up on a few rules. Your life is good, but could be better.

Score 5: Danger! Danger! Warning! Warning! (Will Smith) If you slip, you may fall and not be able to get up.

Score 4 or less: You probably already have a guest room in the dog house. You may want to consider tattooing Rules 1, 2 and 3 on your left forearm and Rules 19, 20 and 49 on your right forearm for easy reference. (If you have big forearms, you may want to put more rules on them.)

Summary

Rule 1—When Mama ain't happy, ain't nobody happy.

Rule 2—The rule of two: whenever you do something wrong, you must do the right thing twice for every time you did it wrong to break even.

Rule 3—"Winning" is not a concept that works in marriage.

Rule 4—Whatever chores you do at the beginning of your marriage, plan on doing them for life.

Rule 5—A husband's role in the delivery room is to understand his role in the birthing process is not important relative to his wife's and that he needs to spend the rest of his life making restitution for that fact.

Rule 6—Going shopping with your wife is like being seventeen during election year. You can have all the opinions you want, but you can't vote.

Rule 7—There is no such thing as women's work. There is work that is shared, and then there is men's work.

Rule 8—When looking at other women, the three-second rule applies.

Rule 9—Never whistle while you pack.

Rule 10—Put the toilet seat down, but not the lid.

Rule 11—The total purchase cost for your wife's new clothes must include the money to take your wife out to show them off.

Rule 12—If you buy a gift for your wife that you can use, it doesn't count.

Rule 13—If you buy your wife a gift and give it to her one week or more ahead of the occasion, it doesn't count.

Rule 14—When a man buys something that is not a joint purchase decision, you have just given your wife permission to spend at least double that amount.

Rule 15—When buying something for the household that can be shared, it will be considered your purchase.

Rule 16—Outside of special occasions, a small gift for your wife counts the same as a large gift.

Rule 17—If your wife buys you a gift that you don't care for, give a strong appearance of appreciation.

Rule 18—On romantic holidays, do not include, "What's for dinner?" in your salutation.

Rule 19—If your children ask your permission, and you ask them what Mama said, ask Mama anyway, regardless of what they say.

Rule 20—Allow your wife to talk twice as much as you. She knows that you only listen to half of what she says.

Rule 21—Ask directions, even if you think you may be able to find your way.

Rule 22—Read the instructions, even if you don't need to.

Rule 23—Always anticipate your wife's needs, unless she doesn't want you to.

Rule 24—When you hear your wife singing her own praises, it's a good indication that you aren't doing it enough.

Rule 25—When your wife says, "You will be sorry if you..." Don't interpret this as a veiled warning; take it as a promise.

Rule 26—Your wife will always hear what you say (whether she is there or not), so be flattering and positive.

Rule 27—Even in a pair of dirty jeans, see the beauty of your wife.

Rule 28—When referring to your wife's age, use the following: (1) If your wife is younger, the term to use is "much younger," (2) If your wife is your age, use "younger," (3) If your wife is older, she is "my age."

Rule 29—A few gray hairs on your wife should be considered invisible. Any more than those are "natural highlights."

Rule 30—When all else fails, throw yourself at the mercy of your wife.

Rule 31—When planning to do home projects, plan on doing all of the work yourself, unless your wife doesn't want you to.

Rule 32—Your wife never looks fat.

Rule 33—Remember that your greatest achievements are always due to your wife's support.

Rule 34—Your relationship with your wife takes precedence over your relationship with your children.

Rule 35—Never let your wife go to bed angry with you. Remember that she is the beneficiary of your life insurance policy.

Rule 36—Never tell your wife that she reminds you of your mother.

Rule 37—Never use the word "fun" when on a business trip.

Rule 38—When people compliment you about your children, attribute those good graces to your wife.

Rule 39—If people complain about your children, attribute those bad graces to yourself.

Rule 40—Remember to thank your in-laws for raising such a wonderful daughter.

Rule 41—Remember that all that you have, you share, unless it's hers.

Rule 42—Let your wife start getting dressed first. It's your job to coordinate your clothes with hers.

Rule 43—When discussing colors, scents or textures, your wife is more precise than you are.

Rule 44—When decorating your home, the best you can hope for is to have input into one room.

Rule 45—When deciding on a house to buy, choose the one your wife likes.

Rule 46—Vacation for your wife means no children.

Rule 47—Tell your wife that you love her at least three times each day. Keep a tally sheet in your pocket, if necessary.

Rule 48—When ordering your meal, order food that your wife will enjoy. It will make the meal more enjoyable.

Rule 49—When your wife is setting you up, you can't act like you know you are being set up.

Rule 50—When newly married, you will be asked by your friends how you like being married. The best response to this is, "If I had known marriage was going to be this good, I would have married my wife much earlier."

Rule 51—Always compliment your wife's cooking. It will save you from going hungry.

Rule 52—Remember that marriage is not 50/50, it's 100/100.

Warning—These rules may change without notice, at the option of your wife.

Conclusion—Teach your children these rules from birth.

OUR LATEST "MAMA" PRODUCT . . .

"Mama's Greeting Cards"

GET A SET OF 10 CARDS WITH

5 OF MAMA'S FAVORITE RULES

FOR *only* $12.95 (PLUS $1 SHIPPING)

Orders will be processed upon receipt of payment.
Please make payments payable in U. S. dollars.
Please allow 2-3 weeks for shipping.

YES! Please send me "Mama's Greeting Cards" at $12.95 per set.

Quantity _____
S&H ($1/set) _____
TOTAL _____

Please send check or money order to:

DESTINATION PUBLICATIONS
9050 N Capitol of TX. Hwy
Bldg. 3, Suite 180
Austin, Texas 78727